HUAN TALKS

ALLAN ANDREWS

Made with ♥ on the Notion Press Platform
www.notionpress.com

For all the true hearts who have inspired...

Contents

Contents

Contents

Muse Voice

"Do not be afraid, little flock, for it is your Father's good pleasure to give you the kingdom. The Kingdom of God is not coming with things that can be observed; nor will they say, 'Look, here it is! ' or 'There it is! ' For, in fact, the Kingdom of God is among you"

~ Bible

1. Letter Two

Dear J, K, L, M, N and O

The family chain is broken in the world to get reunited with an unbreakable strength. Subject is a verb. It is a three syllable word.

Yours Sincerely

With Love

Allan Andrews

2. Rat's Childhood

Long lost childhood days,
I.T recalled with tears.

Those days were lost,
That made I.T worse.
I.T got no toys but had fear of –
Tools that worked for selfish beings.
They stole I.T's life and childhood,
Hunger was I.T's only friend.
I.T is a being;
Being is called it…

3. Some get swept away...

Time and nature write
Words of grief and joy;
They form life upright
With their wit of joy.
Some get swept away
By the time's passage;
Still their memories stay
As life's bright image.
All we love will say adieu
When their time arrives;
Still, we need to get through…
That is what life needs.

4. War

Every war sings a worse music;
A Mournful voice forms its lyrics.
Machine guns make sound of drum;
Anger makes all songs come.
Women and children form chores;
Death always rests in songs.
How far we live, no one knows
Still we sing the war's own songs.

5. Thalassophile

In the night of stars
Within the midnight…
Standing and staring sea
Helps her soul to flee;
Never has she ever bored,
Never has she ever tired.
Sea has a great magic,
On its music's peak;
That mesmerises her soul
From deep to soul's whole.
Sight of sea has an art,
That heals the pain of hearts.
She always wonder;
How is the sea being a healer?
Maybe it's because,
Sea knows all the cause…

6. Flow

From walks of life
Bright colours call
To blind his eyes
With beautiful lies
He paints the first
Saying it's fine…
Then by thinking
It's okay to be so…
Finally believing
Everything happens…
So he moves on…
Now matters now.

7. Choice Matters

Deep and abiding hell
In the mind she bears
Then comes the calm
But it's late for her...
Maybe it's its style.
Drinks from both cup
Her mind feels both...
Happy in life, she is
That makes her flow
But drought eats her
Maybe it's its style.
Dare to live, she leaves
It sounds bitter good
But it's better choice
For, beauty remains
Amidst the disorder
That's how it was & is...
Maybe it's its style.

8. The Black Cap Girl

Like a wind of joy
Her smile comes
From her tiny eyes.
Depth of curiosity,
She hides within her.
She is an answer;
Of beauty and truth.
There's something,
Something she trusts
Remains within her.
Let the world never…
Steal it…let the world.
A human, she is…
Her soul's mind speaks
From the very beginning…
And she knows it's love
Love that abides…
For, she is the star
Of the man who is being.
So, I write with my soul;
On her, in her, from her…

9. Embrace New

Being the being of being..
Being the love of being
Not all things need search
Something needs it
To embrace new truths
Of now and each now…
Like simile's simile
Some hearts speak,
Some hearts sing.
There come the labels!
Of judging words
Those words are fake
But bear lovely mask
No one to blame
For not knowing it.
Bias is a fiction
Written by fools.

10. Water's Thirst

Soul of her heart's heart
Feels the dark cool breeze
Hardly finds the meaning
To remain in and on…
Enters the Indifference;
Walk away from Love.
Through raining sighs
Her eyes make cries
Staying in lake
Still thirsty days make…
Trapped in thoughts
Her free bird mind…

11. Truths

Blind are the metaphors
Blind are the similes
Those fall out of logic
When speaking of a thought.
Feelings are greater
Still it's true.
Truth isn't this but these;
Yes, it's plural for wise.
Singular for babies;
Truth becomes narrow.

12. Tears

Some feelings are stealers
Steal them thy eye's eye
Tears can regain
A way to come back
Good companions they're…
Come at the right time.
Heal and keep you calm
Leave without adieu
Don't thank them we too
No sorrow they have
Take part in ours
For ever and ever.

13. Nothing

They said nothing & nothing…
Nothing became something.
Where there is nothing,
Is there really nothing?
Role of zero, plays nothing
And there is something.
Void means nothing;
Still it plays a role…
Nothing is nothing;
Nothingness is something.
Something we remain
From nothing we are
Nothing makes our fancy
Fancy nothing we make
Unsteady nothing is a thing
That's born from a big thing
That's not really nothing
Nothing can be far-fetched
And there is really nothing
Between being & non-being

14. Maybe

Maybe my thoughts thy feelings
Maybe thy feelings my thoughts
Still, we are Hu beings.
Part of soil we are Tagged with labels…
From birth to D-day
Let it be but it's not us;
Days of starless nights…
Bear together we live
Part of the soil we are.
A way ahead we see with-
Being in the woods of thoughts.
Use things we Hu beings
Things do use us all the time.
No escape exists to exit out
But all the way we strive
To come out of imagination
None can give us handy truths
Make it handy with some paint.
Pre-written scripts we bear
Stagnation is resignation.

15. Ancient Widow

All things' absence
Creates a void to fill
Within space & time;
As a relic she remains.
Slowly it happens
Like withering flowers
Loved and dear ones,
All deny their existence
Some do it knowingly
Some unknowingly do
Still she has to live
In wood's soul ways…
Her voice, unheard;
Her mind, unknown.
Entropy reigns life
Still she dares to live
Ahead and ahead;
To the unknown end.

16. Moments

Some thoughts can yell
Silently with violent tune
Of death and life
That foster curiosity
To know the unknown
Ends of solitude of days.
Some words can speak
Without any letters
Of the moving dialects.
From the evergreen
Lands of mystery
They speak the diction.
Some songs can sing,
Like a soft kiss and hug,
With the lyrics of silence
That forms & makes joy
Which words can't describe
That's the beauty of peace.

17. Life

Every day has paints
Time is its canvas
One colours it well
Ends with joy at night.
One sells the paintings
To reach the mornings
Love is the single brush
One has forever and ever
Some paintings look empty
Some are just fine
Some are mesmerising
Life is for living with life.

18. Irony

Together in dream we live
Alone in reality we survive
Together in life we exist
Alone in reality we thrive
Not to be described highly;
All offer witty thoughts
To sate the thirst of mind.
Stories never end…
Songs never stop…
Mirth & merry we seek
Amidst the colours of life
Calming green is yelling now
Few cares the irony…
A few knows what's not…

19. Parasitic Hopes

Beware of the hopes…
Some are brutally fake.
Like a giant swallows food
Those hopes swallow rights;
Feelings are first swallowed
Frozen thoughts for dinner…
All know but none reacts…
Maybe light's blindness rules…
Running beings are dead now!
Come & eat them, folly Hopes.
Still there are some true hopes
Hopes with blood, flesh and life…
Songs are heard from them
But they don't talk or speak
They don't know to speak
Nothing but songs they sing…

20. Hate

Hate is nothing but hate
Hate is something great.
Ellipsis is the only rescue…
Oh holy poesy of life, I seek
Crack, break, tear & blow me
Blow to thy healing thoughts
Tear into feathers of secret
Break away from ravings
Crack the wall of ignorance.
Hate is a call to change…

21. Coffee Night

Opening her eyes,
She saw Eric Arthur Blair
He said to her, "All are equal
But some are more equal."
She replied him, "All are animals
But some are more animals."
They had a coffee together.
There she saw Edgar Allan Poe.
He told her, "She was watching…
A dream within a dream…"

22. Thieves

When he was out of his home,
A group of common thieves
Came to his home.
They stole his things
But left him with his choices.
When he was out of his mind,
A group of brutally selfish thieves
Came to his mind.
They stole his choices
But left him with his things.
...She replied him, "All are animals
But some are more animals..."

23. Crowd Echoes

Sometimes some speak;
Sometimes some don't...
Fear none but echoes
For that's sharp as a knife...
Echoes of the majority
Can be killers of truth.
Echoes of the majority
Can be clappers of truth.
Fear none but echoes
For that's sharp as a knife...

24. Colours Of Cold

Falls humour into brain,
I'm out of myself…
Sometimes things change
From a wide range & space.
Deathly but deathless, hunts
Lively but lifeless, lives…
When towers bridge to cold,
Yelling not to be a mad dog.
Comes from half closed eyes;
That's not a night world.
Call it a room but I don't see
Me or anyone but I see…
Empty blank page of my brain
Drawing myself without ink…
Me not to the good night hours –
Of deep songs' shower
Of voice I hear from thee
Me not to the beauty –
Of anything around…
Filling myself with the cool's hot.
Let me be the colours of cold
Let me be the hardness of rock…

Let's don't care the pictures of life…
Life is aimlessly beautiful & bitter…

25. Holy Love

Mountains have stories
Of the unknown hermits…
They threw their humane
From the body they live
They sought to know
Deep feelings of beauty…
Everything they sought
And regained spirit…
Mountains have stories
Of the unknown hermits…
Let's give children of truth
With beauty of known truths…

26. Mom's Lament

Once,
Without bags, my child lived
Without shoes, my child smiled
Without dresses, my child giggled
My child wanted me and milk.
Then,
Two sellers came to me
They forced me to buy
Some identity cards
They gave that to my child.
Later,
My child is no more…

27. Murder

They have killed her
And entombed her
In their two words...
Both words have dead children;
Out of nothing they form sane & insane.
Then they seek & long for her;
And she is deaf to their plea.
For, they've buried her in two words:
GOOD & BAD are those two words.

28. Learner

Be not a slave
Be not a student
Be not a disciple
Be a learner
Learner of life.
Life will move hearts
To great oceans of notions.
Be still and alive
To learn each lessons
Life may show some masters
Know their philosophies;
Add some question tags to it…
Thee don't be their slaves
These don't be their disciples.
Take their questions;
Not their thoughts.

29. Autumn

When all leaves fall
He lost his whole body.
He feel to yell
As he is in hell.
Wind takes up dust;
Dust in the heart's nest.
Then it makes dry,
Tears in his eye.
Smile is a bliss;
Comes like a kiss.
Still in autumn,
Heart has that hymn.

30. Death

An end or a beginning of sales…
A renewal to reconnect…
A means to disperse & transform…
A fantasy of the forms that exist…
When he comes to that moment;
I am no more, Nor dead.
My form splits…I'm not there
Again everything restarts…
With my unanswered questions..!

31. Words

Words are filled…
With plenty of strikes
Multiple eyes see
Multiple realities…
A single word can be
Thy garden and forest…

32. Magic of Colours

Quest for the magic of colours,
Shows him the colours' greatness.
From the beginning to the infinity,
Colours have got their mysteries.
Light is the mother of colours;
Father is our mother nature.
There comes the first magic;
Our mother is father to colours.
Second magic happens in art;
Colours become the creator
Of light and beauty of nature.
Creator and creature unite…
To deepen others beauty;
Colours paint themselves.
There ensues the third magic;
Colours remould themselves.
Every mind has colours
Thoughts are the true colours.
There lies the fourth magic;
Colours unite the human minds.
Every life has its colours;
One who lives a worthy life,

Paints a great art in life's canvas.
There arises colours' final magic…

33. He Lives

With intuitions and fear…he lives
Lost dreams shine in his sad eyes.
Bears all complaints…he lives.
Only he knows his feelings better…
Being a peacemaker…he lives.
He finds no peace but he lives
He has no name to bear;
Better to call him city dove.

34. For Thee…

Beauty never ends in you;
In wit you spread your hue.
More than your shining eyes,
Love falls for your wise visions.
When my thoughts fall apart,
Your words awaken your mind.
I seek you as my Muse
For writing all my verses.
As raindrops fill the grassy field
I feel thy coolness in my mind.
Draping myself in thy aroma
Adorns my way to ink thy soul…

35. Pen & Paper

Pen says to paper,
You are my canvas in life.
I seek your friendship,
To enter hearts of people;
By inking my thoughts in you.
Paper says to pen,
I love to be your canvas.
Softly kiss my heart;
By your hearty witty words.
I shall keep your words in heart.

36. Nonsense & Sense

She worked for years
She gained positions
She hid your ignorance
Let her take rest
Send her to the infirmary…
To rest in peace…
They worked for years
They didn't bother positions
They are whistleblowers
Let them take charge
Send them to power
Give them a room in brain
Write their name in upper case
Write that in thy mind: 'Fantasy'…

37. A Child's Cry

What if you are a mother
Who wants to milk her child
When thousand calls come
And thy lovely child cries…
A child is not just human
It's something that longs…
Longs for your care
For, it lacks strength…
My child is my poems & art;
I milk them with my soul…

38. She remains sad & still

Fools go behind the force,
Like the stray dogs run.
She remains sad and still…
All seek a good man
To throw and show
The unending anger…
They being the voice
And for a purpose;
She remains sad and still.
He remains cold and still…

39. Two In One

A poet cries and writes…
His tears water and ink
To the unknown hearts of brains
He is a mother who sings
Melodies for his child
His child sings his sorrows
His child sings his joys
They live in a world of words
Then to them, words talk…
He can understand;
Somebody who is nobody–
That's the ultimate irony…

40. Last Chance

There is a last chance
For, there is an end.
But the whole & all flow…
So, there is no end.
All love to flow-
Flow with life's tide.
And some only flow;
Rest are in rest.
Some rest in shadows;
Some rest in dream web.
Shadows make eyes blind…
Dream web traps movement…
These stop life's flow.
So, let's be in light;
That is in the present..!

41. Dream

Nothing gets fulfilled
In the hands of tomorrow
Work becomes real today
Then let it be a story
Without leaving heart to dry
Dreams be not mirage
Instead let it transform;
To keep you far ahead
By better thoughts.
Let "Why" seek you
Not you to "Whys"
You be with "Hows"
Thus life is better.

42. Ringing Myth

All have started with 24 bells
That halos and echoes at first
Then comes the duties of myth
Then comes the norms of myth
Then comes the trap of myth
Full of myth life holds us in link
The first half seems to be fun
And the myth of time run ruins
The life from its love and core
There the second phase begins
With the lifeless D-living run
Hands full of long lost days
24 bells ring for namesake…
Mind doubts the will & choices.

43. He, The Shepherd

In him thee see mom
In him thee see dad
In him thee see truth
Not like modern ones
Of ninety nine sheeps.
In him thee see way
In him thee see light
In him thee see hope
Not like modern ones
Of ninety nine sheeps.
In him thee see courage
In him thee see power
In him thee see love
Not like modern ones
Of ninety nine sheeps.
Thou needn't wonder
He is the one who dares
To seek that single lamb
Leaving the ninety nine...

44. City

A city never sees stars
Gets banned his nights & peace
Empty lights, it sells…
Where he sees him in bliss once,
Is taken away from him now.
He misses his silence & him…
He misses his home and room...

45. Unheard Truth

Tick Tick Tick
Gap is shortening
Clock is yelling
Still he sees me in…
Down the way opens
To the unknown far
Have to move on & on…
To the best of my ends
To the best sip of wine.
Untold stories I have
Unheard songs I owe
Thus my dear he goes
To the right and left…
Unending & unknown
Mysteries form beauty.
All things are not thine
And it's not for thee
Things are not to hill
And it's to live and feel
Pleasure you gain is true
Find your feeling's truth
Thy brain is not the end…

46. Huan Being

A huan is a blank canvas by birth;
Pure as a precious pearl.
Conservatives draw on and on;
Pictures of walls and borders.
Alas, the canvas is spoiled…
Fire of grief catches the canvas;
Turn the canvas into ashes.
All think it's the end, but not.
From there raises a Huan Being;
With the wings of peace & love.

47. The Day

'Kill me before the day,
Or you will regret...'
She wrote that sentence
On herself and slept
In her basement
In Darlington.
That was a letter to him
For her dearest James.
Some letters are not to be posted
Just to be written...as she did...

48. Why thee hurt?

Oh sadness, my sadness
Why thee hurt me…
Why without reason, thee hurt,
Am I thy playing cards?
Silence, silence, silence…
Sadness starts to speak :
'I am what you are.
What creates & gives you life
Gives me too the life & beauty;
One with the whole, I do seek…'

49. He

Speaks his mind in silence
Beware of the coincidence
Myth is thicker than water.
Mind tunes him into its ways
He doesn't fall into its trap
Myth is thicker than blood…

50. Name is a myth…

The way I've talked
Can make thee doubt…
Whether I know you
Before our eyes've met.
Yes, I know thee for long;
From my dreams of words.
And thy name is different;
Eyes are same with depths,
Feelings are same with tears,
Mind has miles to go & reach…
Name is a myth, let's say…
Name is a myth, let's sing…

51. Star & Sun

Why thee born so early?
And me so late for thee…
Dear night's gentle star
I come to thee my way…
My love is love that lives
Forever within your heart
And thee within my core
Dear night's gentle star
Why thee born so early?
And me so late for thee…

52. Medicine

Your medicine, I am
Eat me my Love of life
I remain to your heart
With truth of love & wit
No words make thee
No songs sing thee
And my heart does
Well it does in love
By never ending feel
That ties stars to night.

53. Bonding

An early bird he is…
Loves in rainbow
They live together
A Night owl she is…
Loves in rainbow
They exist together.
When he is a sea;
She has become sky.
When he is a sky;
She has become sea.
His medicine, she is…
Each other, they heal.
Their love is love;
Forever and ever.

54. That Girl

That girl, she was once…
Running & chasing flies
Butterflies & dragonflies;
But nothing she could.
All of a sudden it happened
All chase and run stopped;
A flower plant, she became.
All flies started to dance
Around her petals and leaves.
All, whole, that's all about her…

55. Seasons

He believes in seasons
Autumn is his fave
He believes in change
Let rain rain & fall
Beauty of nature
Includes huans too
In a nutshell, to sing
Life has taught him
Three musical words
Think, Wait, Accept…

56. Snow Love

Soul… Rock… Soil…
World of dreams
And sorrows to share…
So many ways we merge
Into the depths of the heart
Of the infinite…here you and I
Are not; but life filled
In the moments.
We are together…
Words are limited…
Creating we in us;
We exist in us…

57. Drops

Keeping herself in exile,
She represses her inner aisle..
To someone or anyone
But she sees no one…
She sees darkness
Where she is lifeless.
Live, survive or just existing
What is rhyming…
She remembers something,
Which is not just a thing;
An old friend's hearty talk-
'Everything is a part of life's walk.'

58. Story Sings

Friendship inspired ink to flow
Ink became the words of soul
The soul became the colours of life
Life became the art of love…
He entered through the first door;
Came back with empty hands,
Entered through the second door;
Came back with her and him.
She entered through the third door
Came back with two children.

59. Rain and Train

They became parent
Of two children
From them came…
Rain and Train
The flesh of their heart
The blood of their soul
First seeds from chaos
Tigers of light and joy
With burning hearts.
Beauty and truth
Transformed the souls.
Their mother is a woman
Who knows the Sun…
Who wears the Sun.

60. World of Us…

Did you eat breakfast?
"Yes, she had it
Early in the morning",
He replied.
To be continued;
By the second one.

61. Letter One

Dear J, K, L, M, N and O

It is a single syllable word . Noun is an adjective. The family chain is broken in this world to get reunited with an unbreakable strength.

Yours Sincerely

With Love

Allan Andrews

And It Goes...

Written during the days of solitude...

9 798890 027948

Printed by Libri Plureos GmbH in Hamburg, Germany